Praise for *Appalachian Elegy: Poetry and Place*

"'I will guide you,' bell hooks promises, and delivers, in her remarkable collection, Appalachian Elegy. In meditations intimate and clear, with 'radical grace,' she negotiates 'beauty and danger,' the animal and human worlds, the pain of history, the dead and the living. With wisdom and courage, she moves through lamentation to resurrection, and the worlds she unearths are an 'avalanche of splendor.'"

—Paula Bohince, author of *The Children* and
Incident at the Edge of Bayonet Woods

"Hush arbors were safe places in the deep woods where slaves could commune with each other to lift their choral voices to the heavens as they tarried for freedom. bell hooks comes from a people who deeply connected with this country's 'backwoods' and hills in Kentucky and decided to stead in these spaces. Tending and tilling the land that afforded them independence and the freedom to unmask in isolation. They were 'renegades and rebels' who didn't seek to civilize Kentucky's wilds, instead developing a besidedness with the land that informs bell hooks's sense of self and belonging. This collection of poems is a departure for the important polemicist, a place where she is able to roam her boundless imagination using her emotional intelligence as her primary compass. Praise songs for her ancestors sit beside her meditations on turtles. Here is a rare glance into the soul of our beloved, prolific, yet private bell hooks, who took her mother's surname as her nom de plume. Here she returns to her mother's woods, to the 'wilderness within.'"

—dream hampton, journalist and filmmaker

"The collection reflects aesthetic and linguistic choices based on the thinking and feeling of someone who has made important contributions to contemporary thought and who thinks and feels deeply about what Kentucky—as 'here' and home—means to her."

—Edwina Pendarvis, Professor Emeritus at Marshall University
and author of *Like the Mountains of China*

Praise for *Appalachian Elegy: Poetry and Place,* continued

"bell hooks has crafted a lyrical, sweeping panorama, deftly conjuring the tangled root and insistent steam of Appalachia. In these lean, melodic poems, she holds the land close; it's achingly apparent how essential these memories are to the raw, unleashed spirit that typifies her body of work. These communiqués, from an elsewhere the mind visits too rarely, reside in that constantly shifting space between melancholy and celebration. No one but bell hooks could have taken us there."

—Patricia Smith, four-time National Poetry Slam
individual champion

Appalachian Elegy

Appalachian Elegy

Poetry and Place

bell hooks

UNIVERSITY PRESS OF KENTUCKY

Copyright © 2012 by Gloria Jean Watkins (bell hooks)

Published by the University Press of Kentucky
Scholarly publisher for the Commonwealth,
serving Bellarmine University, Berea College, Centre
College of Kentucky, Eastern Kentucky University,
The Filson Historical Society, Georgetown College,
Kentucky Historical Society, Kentucky State University,
Morehead State University, Murray State University,
Northern Kentucky University, Transylvania University,
University of Kentucky, University of Louisville,
and Western Kentucky University.

Editorial and Sales Offices: The University Press of Kentucky
663 South Limestone Street, Lexington, Kentucky 40508-4008
www.kentuckypress.com

16 15 14 13 12   5 4 3 2 1

Library of Congress Cataloging-in-Publication Data
hooks, bell.
  Appalachian elegy : poetry and place / bell hooks.
     p.   cm.
  Includes index.
  ISBN 978-0-8131-3669-1 (pbk. : alk. paper) — ISBN 978-0-8131-3670-7 (pdf) —
ISBN 978-0-8131-4076-6 (epub)
  1. hooks, bell—Childhood and youth—Poetry. 2. Appalachian Region—
Poetry. 3. Kentucky—Poetry. I. Title.
  PS3608.O594A84 2012
  811'.6—dc23
                                    2012018046

This book is printed on acid-free paper meeting
the requirements of the American National Standard
for Permanence in Paper for Printed Library Materials.

Manufactured in the United States of America.

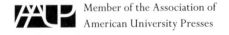 Member of the Association of
            American University Presses

Contents

Introduction: On Reflection and Lamentation   1

Appalachian Elegy   9

Index of First Lines   77

Introduction

On Reflection and Lamentation

Sublime silence surrounds me. I have walked to the top of the hill, plopped myself down to watch the world around me. I have no fear here, in this world of trees, weeds, and growing things. This is the world I was born into: a world of wild things. In it the wilderness in me speaks. I am wild. I hear my elders caution mama, telling her that she is making a mistake, letting me "run wild," letting me run with my brother as though no gender separates us. We are making our childhood together in the Kentucky hills, experiencing the freedom that comes from living away from civilization. Even as a child I knew that to be raised in the country, to come from the backwoods, left one without meaning or presence. Growing up we did not use terms like "hillbilly." Country folk lived on isolated farms away from the city; backwoods folks lived in remote areas, in the hills and hollers.

To be from the backwoods was to be part of the wild. Where we lived, black folks were as much a part of the wild, living in a natural way on the earth, as white folks. All backwoods folks were poor by material standards; they knew how to make do. They were not wanting to tame the wildness, in themselves or nature. Living in the Kentucky hills was where I first learned the importance of being wild.

1

Later, attending college on the West Coast, I would come to associate the passion for freedom and the wildness I had experienced as a child with anarchy, with the belief in the power of the individual to be self-determining. Writing about the connection between environments, nature, and creativity in the introduction to *A Place in Space,* Gary Snyder states: "Ethics and aesthetics are deeply intertwined. Art, beauty, and craft have always drawn on the self-organizing 'wild' side of language and mind. Human ideas of place and space, our contemporary focus on watersheds, become both models and metaphors. Our hope would be to see the interacting realms, learn where we are, and thereby move towards a style of planetary and ecological cosmopolitanism." Snyder calls this approach the "practice of the wild," urging us to live "in the self-disciplined elegance of 'wild' mind." By their own practice of living in harmony with nature, with simple abundance, Kentucky black folks who lived in the backwoods were deeply engaged with an ecological cosmopolitanism. They fished; hunted; raised chickens; planted what we would now call organic gardens; made homemade spirits, wine, and whiskey; and grew flowers. Their religion was interior and private. Mama's mama, Baba, refused to attend church after someone made fun of the clothes she was wearing. She reminded us that God could be worshipped everyday, anywhere. No matter that they lived according to Appalachian values, they did not talk about themselves as coming from Appalachia. They did not divide Kentucky into East and West. They saw themselves as renegades and rebels, folks who did not want to be hemmed in by rules and laws, folks that wanted to remain independent. Even when circumstances forced them out of the country into the city, they were still wanting to live free.

As there were individual black folks who explored the regions of this nation before slavery, the first black Appalachians being fully engaged with the Cherokee, the lives of most early black Kentuckians were shaped by a mixture of free sensibility and slave mentality. When slavery ended in Kentucky, life was hard for the vast majority of black people as white supremacy and racist domination did not end. But those folks who managed to own land, especially land in isolated country sites or hills (sometimes inherited from white folks for whom they had worked for generations, or sometimes purchased), were content to be self-defining and self-determining even if it meant living with less. No distinctions were made between those of us who dwelled in the hills of eastern or western Kentucky. Our relatives from eastern Kentucky did not talk about themselves as Appalachians, and in western Kentucky we did not use the term; even if one lived in the hills where the close neighbors were white and hillbilly, black people did not see themselves as united with these folk, even though our habits of being and ways of thinking were more like these strangers than those of other black folks who lived in the city—especially black folks who had money and urban ways. In small cities and towns, the life of a black coal miner in western Kentucky was more similar to the life of an Eastern counterpart than different. Just as the lives of hillbilly black folks were the same whether they lived in the hills of eastern or western Kentucky.

In the Kentucky black subcultures, folks were united with our extended kin, and our identities were more defined by labels like "country" and "backwoods." It was not until I went away to college that I was questioned about Appalachia, about hillbilly culture, and it was always assumed by these faraway outsiders that only poor white people lived in the backwoods and in the hills. No wonder then that black folks who cherish our past, the independence that characterized our backwoods ancestors, seek to recover and restore their history, their legacy. Early on in my life I learned from those Kentucky backwoods elders, the folks whom we might now label "Appalachian," a set of values rooted in the belief that above all else one must be self-determining. It is the foundation that is the root of my radical critical consciousness. Folks from the backwoods were certain about two things: that every human soul needed to be free and that the responsibility of being free required one to be a person of integrity, a person who lived in such a way that there would always be congruency between what one thinks, says, and does.

These ancestors had no interest in conforming to social norms and manners that made lying and cheating acceptable. More often than not, they believed themselves to be above the law whenever the rules of so-called civilized culture made no sense. They farmed, fished, hunted, and made their way in the world. Sentimental nostalgia does not call me to remember the worlds they invented. It is just a simple fact that without their early continued support for dissident thinking and living, I would not have been able to hold my own in college and beyond when conformity promised to provide me with a sense of safety and greater regard. Their "Appalachian values," imprinted on my consciousness as core truths I must live by, provided and continue to provide me with the tools I needed and need to survive whole in a postmodern world.

Living by those values, living with integrity, I am able to return to my native place, to an Appalachia that is no longer silent about its diversity or about the broad sweep of its influence. While I do not claim an identity as Appalachian, I do claim a solidarity, a sense of belonging, that makes me one with the Appalachian past of my ancestors: black, Native American, white, all "people of one blood" who made homeplace in isolated landscapes where they could invent themselves, where they could savor a taste of freedom.

In my latest collection of essays, *Writing Beyond Race,* I meditate for page after page on the issue of where it is black folk may go to be free of the category of race. Ironically, the segregated world of my Kentucky childhood was the place where I lived beyond race. Living my early childhood in the isolated hills of Kentucky, I made

4

a place for myself in nature there—roaming the hills, walking the fields hidden in hollows where my sharecropper grandfather Daddy Gus planted neat rows of growing crops. Without evoking a naïve naturalism that would suggest a world of innocence, I deem it an act of counterhegemonic resistance for black folks to talk openly of our experiences growing up in a southern world where we felt ourselves living in harmony with the natural world.

To be raised in a world where crops grown by the hands of loved ones is to experience an intimacy with earth and home that is lost when everything is out there, somewhere away from home, waiting to be purchased. Since much sociological focus on black experience has centered on urban life—lives created in cities— little is shared about the agrarian lives of black folk. Until Isabel Wilkerson published her awesome book *The Warmth of Other Suns,* which documents the stories of black folks leaving agrarian lives to migrate to cities, there was little attention paid to the black experience of folks living on the land. Just as the work of the amazing naturalist George Washington Carver is often forgotten when lists are made of great black men. We forget our rural black folks, black farmers, folks who long ago made their homes in the hills of Appalachia.

All my people come from the hills, from the backwoods, even the ones who ran away from this heritage refusing to look back. No one wanted to talk about the black farmers who lost land to white supremacist violence. No one wanted to talk about the extent to which that racialized terrorism created a turning point in the lives of black folks wherein nature, once seen as a freeing place, became a fearful place. That silence has kept us from knowing the ecohistories of black folks. It has kept folk from claiming an identity and a heritage that is so often forgotten or erased.

It is no wonder, then, that when I returned to my native state of Kentucky after more than thirty years of living elsewhere, memories of life in the hills flooded my mind and heart. And I could see the link between the desecration of the land as it was lived on by red and black folk and the current exploitation and destruction of our environment. Coming home to Kentucky hills was, for me, a way to declare allegiance to environment struggles aimed at restoring proper stewardship to the land. It has allowed me to give public expression to the ecofeminism that has been an organic part of my social action on behalf of peace and justice.

In *Longing For Running Water: Ecofeminism and Liberation*, theologian Ivone Gebara contends: "The ecofeminist movement does not look at the connection between the domination of women and of nature solely from the perspective of cultural ideology and social structures; it seeks to introduce new ways of thinking that are more at the service of ecojustice." In keeping with this intent, in the preface to *Belonging: A Culture of Place*, where I make a space for the ecofeminist within me to speak, I conclude with this statement: "I pay tribute to the past as a resource that can serve as a foundation for us to revision and renew our commitment to the present, to making a world where all people can live fully and well, where everyone, can belong."

The joyous sense of homecoming that I experience from living in Kentucky does not change the reality that it has been difficult for black rural Kentuckians to find voice, to speak our belonging. Most important, it has been difficult to speak about past exploitation and oppression of people and land, to give our sorrow words. Those of us who dare to talk about the pain inflicted on red and black folks in this country, connecting that historical reality to the pain inflicted on our natural world, are often no longer silenced; we are simply ignored. It is the recognition of that pain that causes a constant mourning.

My cries of lamentation faintly echo the cries of freedom fighter Sojourner Truth, who often journeyed deep into the forest to loudly lament the pain of slavery, the pain of having no voice. Truth spoke to the trees, telling them, "when I cried out with a mother's grief none but Jesus heard." When I first walked on the hills belonging to me I felt an overwhelming sense of triumph. I felt that I could reclaim a place in this Kentucky landscape in the name of all the displaced Native Americans, African Americans, and all the black Indians (who cannot "prove" on paper that they are who they really are). Chanting with a diverse group of ecofeminist friends, we called forth the ancestors, urging them to celebrate return migration with us. We spread sage, planted trees, and dug holes for blossoming rose bushes in the name of our mother Rosa Bell. I wanted to give her a place to rest in these hills, a place where I can commune with her spirit.

The essays in *Belonging: A Culture of Place* give voice to the collective past of black folks in Kentucky. They include family values that cover the ethics of life in the backwoods and hills of Kentucky. If psychologists are right and there is a core identity imprinted on our souls in her childhood, my soul is a witness to this Kentucky; so it was when I was a child and so it is in my womanhood. My essays are almost always written in clear polemical prose, nothing abstract, nothing mysterious. When poetry stirs in my imagination it is almost always from an indirect place, where language is abstract, where the mood and energy is evocative of submerged emotional intelligence and experience.

Poetry is a useful place for lamentation. Not only the forest Sojourner found solace in, poems are a place where we can cry out. *Appalachian Elegy* is a collection of poems that extend the process of lamentation. Dirge-like at times, the poems repeat sorrow sounds, connecting the pain of a historical Kentucky landscape ravaged by war and all human conditions that are like war. Nowadays we can hear tell of black jockeys, the ones who became famous. But where are the stories of all enslaved black servants who worked with horses, who wanted to mount and ride away from endless servitude? Those stories are silenced. Psychohistory and the power of ways of knowing beyond human will and human reason allow us to re-create, to reimagine. Poems of lamentation allow the melancholic loss that never truly disappears to be given voice. Like a slow solemn musical refrain played again and again, they call us to remember and mourn, to know again that as we work for change our struggle is also a struggle of memory against forgetting.

Appalachian Elegy

1.

hear them cry
the long dead
the long gone
speak to us
from beyond the grave
guide us
that we may learn
all the ways
to hold tender this land
hard clay dirt
rock upon rock
charred earth
in time
strong green growth
will rise here
trees back to life
native flowers
pushing the fragrance of hope
the promise of resurrection

2.

such then is beauty
surrendered
against all hope
you are here again
turning slowly
nature as chameleon
all life change
and changing again
awakening hearts
steady moving from
unnamed loss
into fierce deep grief
that can bear all burdens
even the long passage
into a shadowy dark
where no light enters

3.

night moves
through thick dark
a heavy silence outside
near the front window
a black bear
stamps down plants
pushing back brush
fleeing manmade
confinement
roaming unfettered
confident
any place can become home
strutting down
a steep hill
as though freedom
is all
in the now
no past
no present

4.

earth works
thick brown mud
clinging pulling
a body down
hear wounded earth cry
bequeath to me
the hoe the hope
ancestral rights
to turn the ground over
to shovel and sift
until history
rewritten resurrected
returns to its rightful owners
a past to claim
yet another stone lifted to
throw against the enemy
making way for new endings
random seeds
spreading over the hillside
wild roses
come by fierce wind and hard rain
unleashed furies
here in this untouched wood
a dirge a lamentation
for earth to live again
earth that is all at once a grave
a resting place a bed of new beginnings
avalanche of splendor

5.

small horses ride me
carry my dreams
of prairies and frontiers
where once
the first people roamed
claimed union with the earth
no right to own or possess
no sense of territory
all boundaries
placed by unseen ones
here I will give you thunder
shatter your hearts with rain
let snow soothe you
make your healing water
clear sweet
a sacred spring
where the thirsty
may drink
animals all

6.

listen little sister
angels make their hope here
in these hills
follow me
I will guide you
careful now
no trespass
I will guide you
word for word
mouth for mouth
all the holy ones
embracing us
all our kin
making home here
renegade marooned
lawless fugitives
grace these mountains
we have earth to bind us
the covenant
between us
can never be broken
vows to live and let live

7.

again and again
she calls me
this wilderness within
urging me onward
be here
make a path
where the sound
of ancestors speaks
a language heard beyond the grave
this earth I stand on
belongs to the many dead
treasure I find here
is all gift
tender solace
holding back the future
the dead that will not let us forget
late ones
and even further back
the ancients
dreaming achieving
they will not let us forget
time is aboriginal eternal
they carry us back
take us through the sacred portal
that we may come again then again
into the always present

8.

snow-covered earth
such silence
still divine presence
echoes immortal migrants
all life sustained
darkness comes
suffering touches us
again and again
there is pain
there in the midst of
such harsh barrenness
a cardinal framed in the glass
red light
calling away despair
eternal promise
everything changes and ends

9.

autumn ending
leaves like
fallen soldiers
manmade hard hearts
fighting battles on this once sacred ground
all killing done now
dirt upon dirt
covers all signs of death
memory tamped down
ways to not remember
the disappeared
dying faces
longing to be seen
one lone warrior lives
comes home to the hills
seeking refuge
seeking a place to surrender
the ground where hope remains
and souls surrender

10.

here and there
across and down
treasure uncovered
remnants of ancient ways
not buried deep enough
excavated they surface
objects that say
some part of me
lived here before
reincarnated ancestors
give me breath
urge me—live again
return to familiar ground
hear our lost people speak

11.

no crops grow
when dense clay dirt
packed solid
defies
all manmade
intent to destroy
let a blessing come here
let earth
heal and rejoice
she has here
mother of grace
and constancy
wild roses bloom
scatter these hills
with beauty
that does not linger
offering still the promise of healing
and return

12.

mud sliding down
wet can do this
make danger
fall upon us
turn the pure in heart away
no water for holy cleansing
no water for drying thirst
just black death
smothering earth
soot after fire

13.

wingspan wide
death covers all
prey and predator
turkey buzzards overhead
at the bottom of the hill
no eternity beckons
just ongoing decay
a deep smothering emptiness
profound prolonged lamentation
birds cry high

14.

hard rain
softens harder ground
from solid rock
to mud so thick
feet go under
making every step
dirge and trial
even as joy surfaces
at last today
we plant
we hope

15.

pink and white oleander
not native to Appalachian ground
still here lies
years and years of poison
rebel flags
heritage and hate
in the war to fight hunger and
ongoing loss
there are no sides
there is only
the angry mind of hurt
bringing death too soon
destroying all our dreams
of union

16.

go high up
climb to the very top
look out
remnants of
majesty remain
here where soldiers stand
watching their gods die
what will be given
in return for shelter
an end to hunger
sanctuary
look from the mountaintops
an army of broken promises
land invaded then left
as though there were no other way
to claim belonging

17.

straight ahead
the road curves
signs signal
no motorboats allowed
this lake our water source
let us drink
clear and true
there are swans
resting here magical presence
all reflecting peace

18.

when trees die
all small hearts break
little living creatures
happy and safe
uprooted
now in need of finding
new places
when home
cracks and breaks and falls
all life becomes danger
how to find
another place
where all is not
yet barren

19.

all fields
of tobacco
growing here
gone now
man has made time
take them
surrendered
this harsh crop
to other lands
countries where
the spirit guides
go the way
of lush green
leaving behind
the scent of memory
tobacco leaves
green yellow brown
plant of sacred power
shining beauty
return to Appalachia
make your face known

20.

the glory in old barns
surpassing time
wood gray shadowed black
faded colors
places where painted signs
tell of products
no longer in use
standing or falling down
these structures
carry the weight of history
work done and undone
memories of toil and torment
there was bounty here
tears for sowing
lamentations for the dead
all fragments that remain
remind us
give thanks
gather praise

21.

turtle islands everywhere
heads poking out
bodies embraced in the world
before the coming of the white man
a sea of calm
where turtles rest
on lands breathing life
outside water
that turtles may play
fat succulent slow
enchanting us
with strength to guard and protect
a wall of hardness
store dreams
of a world without humans
a wet world everlasting

22.

sometimes falling rain
carries memories of betrayal
there in the woods
where she was not meant to be
too young she believes
in her right to be free
in her body
free from harm
believing nature
a wilderness she can enter
be solaced
believing the power
that there be sacred place
that there can be atonement now
she returns with no fear
facing the past
ready to risk
knowing these woods now
hold beauty and danger

23.

bring Buddha
to rest home
in Kentucky hills
that outside each window
a light may shine
not a guilt teaching tradition
be balanced
know loving kindness
end suffering
rejoice in the oneness of life
then let go
carry nothing on your back
travel empty
as you climb steep mountain paths

24.

clouds dressed in gray
for mourning
for grief held
white for adoration
dark for sorrow
come soon
an eternity simply hidden
where all sun and glory reigns
even so
in this now
there is just
a promise
of shadows
relentless

25.

soil rich with lime
grass beyond green
turning toward blue
hills of plenty
all but gone
bent under the weight
all human greed
we speak then
tell of a god of miracles
who moves mountains
yet manmade steel
ravishes this earth
all for coal
deep and black
a destiny of burning heat
covering flesh in ash

26.

equine whispering
horses once roaming freely
out in the open
now live enclosed
captured by boundaries of fence and wire
manmade domestication
horses grazing quietly
four-legged buddhas
standing in grace
forgiving

27.

sublime shadows of midnight
bronze brown
in gray white
dappled black beauty
thunder
man of war
a dynasty of flesh
roaming in the mind's eye
pondering
such power harnessed
driven
preyed upon by human
will and desire

28.

morning dawn
mist-covered day
dreaming triumph and victory
horses gather
a herd at the top of the hill
bonded
whispering souls
ready to run
speaking a language only they can hear
sounds beyond
interpretation
no heavy rider's move
in this magic time
no need to tame and mount
all at once
they race
to reach the beyond

29.

softly treading black bear
leaving a trace
green crushed
under innocence
just for now
breaking free
leaving forest for
hill and mountain
fleeing coonskin caps
memories of
renegade red men running
fleeing daniel boone
white wrath
all nature
slaughtered in
the colonizing wake
animals abandoned
alone untouched
sheer good fortune
guides one bear away
a gift of time
with no boundaries
for soon
hunters come
soon comes dying
soon we are captives

30.

burning pain
has its own rhythm
back and back
shaking the foundation of
trees once strong
brought down
by fire
by fierce want
uprooted
all solid
familiar ground
naked now
going once
going twice
leaving damaged
and broken
unending
blackness

31.

returning to sacred places
where all is one
embraced belonging
an intense field of possibility
wondrous goodness
fills the air
grant us great spirits
another chance
to reclaim and nurture earth
glorious sky
divine water
in everyday the blessing of weather
offering change
a constant passing
of life into death
and back again

32.

walking the long way home
walking ever so slow
talking to be
wholly in this world of wonder
standing still
waiting
standing in the center
of a long and winding
dirt road
leading uphill
to a small house
surrounded by lilacs
black-eyed susans
roses and honeysuckle vines
a bench at the bottom
that bodies may rest
before they climb

33.

tap dancing
on tin roofs
heavy rain falls
wetness spreading
all over borders
refusing containment
flash flood warning
sirens call stay in
be still
guard your heart
let rain be
the only necessary movement

34.

fierce winter cold
mind whispers
a lost landscape
telling stories
of how it was then
seated near fire
drinking homemade spirits
sake and brandy wine
spirits bring contentment
for a time
carry us closer
to the sacred
moving through bitterness
our yearning to hold on
to moments of ecstasy
where we imagine
we hear clearly
destiny calling

35.

winds of fate
take the air
push it past the known
in this world of nature
no one can undo
mystery abounds
harsh cold burns skin
fire waits
raging tempests
sweep us
carry us toward
destiny recorded
written down
past present future
change comes

36.

mammoth caves
places alive
before the invention of hours
paleolithic hunters
painting the caves
of lascaux
horses shot with arrows
wild creatures
no longer seen
cave dwellers
searching for sacred paths
then sharing revelation
on these walls
connecting caves
crossing boundaries
of nation and time
bold remains
of untouched history

37.

stained black
Kentucky oak
plank fences
mark boundaries
ghost riders
where the dead live
on the edge of time
slaves worked here
long ago
caressing horse flesh
breathing shared dreams
cared for them
when witnessing
the breaking of yet
another animal spirit
born to be wild and free
a bond forged
whisper to forgotten souls
run run
go as fast as you can
run run
seek an end to bondage

38.

toward light
each bird flies
higher then higher
then swooping down
as though to plummet
as though air a net
to catch and comfort
who can fear
earth
who can fear
sky
when faced with
an infinite possibility
each moment given
a chance to soar
to enter beyond

39.

ritual places
a set offering
dead bird
on wooden slats
carry beauty still
stretched and moaned
as though
bearing its own cross
suffering those last moments
there are altars
in these hills
organic monuments
calling the sacred
rock on which to stand
and know divine presence
witness and testify
as birds of prey
fly high
opening wide wings
reaching past death

40.

on hallowed ground
I cast the circle
that there may be
haven for the lost
refuge and sanctuary
turning to the hills
I place feet on steady ground
letting earth hold me
in praise of air
I lift my hands
to the heavens
call down grace for blessings
for anointed being
turning toward water
I let go remembered sins
cleanse and purify
burning sage
I bring fire to warm
and illuminate
all around this body
light moves
a communion of gathered
spirits

41.

fierce unyielding winds
pressing pushing
against window glass
trees swaying
branches falling
chaos warning
of danger
she does not want
to cut them down
she does not want
to fear those mighty oaks
standing guard
for more years
than can be counted
strong roots sustaining life
holding back
the rush of time
let earth testify
they have the
right to fall
when life comes to an end
to move
in harmony with fate

42.

heavy heart
as fallen snow
bringing behind
wet damp darkness
small dreams
coming true
green coming
from seeds
planted long ago
draw from this
winter death
courage to go on
in the face of white cold
see past this
all-surrounding
whiteness
that beyond
there is hope
that sorrow ends

43.

when the dawn
is still almost dark
I rise restless
watch the
morning come
sly slow
movement into light
from shadow play
an unveiling
inside this dark heart
a yearning to live
as nature lives
surrendering all

44.

fly high
dreaming bird
higher and higher
on the wire of time
no road blocks
no stopping
to think through
why wings flap
what makes
the worthy soar
only this
pure heaven
right now
sky high

45.

barren broken hill
once a place of possibility
now only remnants
old glory gone
heritage sullied with hate
ancestors indigenous and dark
held captive
by soldiers and greed
by bloody conquest
battlefields where the dead live
unclaimed not mourned
histories buried forgotten
lost to a world of cover-ups
ghosts return to these hills
to grieve
cry out lamentations
mourning the desecration
of earthbound bodies
ghosts gather here
make promises
of resurrection and return

46.

overlooking water
I stand
at the top of the hill
looking out
see swans on the lake
grand plumage
more elegant than peacocks
their presence mysterious
all secrecy
how came they
to choose Appalachia
gracing us with their vision
as we climb down
to be close to such beauty
that it may
open our hearts
show us such love
as to offer
no turning back

47.

red beard
strut
strut
wild turkey
congregate
walk in peace
deciduous woodland
undercover
walk to mate
walk to feed
strut
strut
iridescent plumage
moving harem
doing a slow dance
strut
strut

48.

sunken faces
a collapsing gray
shutting down
still bodies
standing in doorways
sitting on
falling-down front porches
on crooked steps
cold now
bone upon bone
outsiders come
taking land
taking life
stripping removing destroying
mountains ravished
leaving in this corrupt wake
souls grieving
earth laments
cries out loud
that justice may come
that it is never too late

49.

with water
anoint the day
all this season
of drought kills
quiet slaughter
effortless
no need to love war
in this space
ongoing silence
absent wetness
call for surrender
for want and thirst
we are brought low
face to face
with essential need
a necessary yearning
we long for rain
for water
to pour into our hearts
an offering of radical grace

50.

all old souls
chant
be tender
walk soft
the bodies of our dead
lie here
wildflowers
red yellow white
adorn memory
pink purple blue
lost in a world of green
all have been
promised
wedded to morning
that will soon come
tears fallen and gone
only faint traces
of grief remain
sorrow lingers
making soil soul deep
our weeping ground

51.

in the gray blue wash of dawn
sacred secrets no longer hidden
make tapestries of repressed memories
soldiers lamenting
the tyranny of war unending
let earth renew
broken spirits
find precious
love once shared
that will not be forgotten
remembered confederates
fugitive desire
past wounds heal
bind broken hearts
give all to glory
beyond country flag nation
yearning for atonement
they bring light
come to early morning fresh

52.

renegades roam here
fugitive longing
darker than night
glorious black bodies
enslaved
with no hope of
belonging
to land
in this new world
of white freedom and flight
some live to die
sleep with no dreams
some find ways
to unravel mysteries
threads of power and domination
a palimpsest of greed
they hope
and hope
for change
find homeplace inside
letting anguish bleed out
make way for new life

53.

blackbirds
come rest home
let your dreaming
winged flying spirits pause
meditate
pause your deep soul be peace
for you can rest here
in this green
enchanted place
claim sanctuary
in these hills
made sacred
by native trust
small yet mighty
find your belonging

54.

burning body of love
no lead turning into gold
flesh only
turning into pain and ash
the bodies and being of old men
coal black skin
soft to touch
smooth as velvet
as kid gloves
they once danced
dreamed themselves
priests and poets all
now they sleep
under loam
rich and generous
as a full heart

55.

take the
hand-me-downs
make do
no culture of poverty
claiming lives here
we a people of plenty
back then
work hard
know no hunger
grow food
sew clothing
build shelter
moonshine still
wine from grape
we a marooned
mountain people
backwoods souls
we know to live on little
to make a simple life
away from manmade
laws and boundaries
spirit guides teach us
offer always
the promise
of an eternal now

56.

star of david
tree of life
double wedding band
a nine patch
such patterns
once shaped our destiny
pieces of cloth
marking a woman's life
sewn together scraps
bits and pieces
tell us life stories
pieced by hand
remnants of passion
an unfulfilled desire
sisters coming together
making peace
offering comfort
ways to warm
to open hearts

57.

fierce grief shadows me
I hold to the memory
of ongoing loss
land stolen bodies shamed
everywhere the stench of
death and retribution
all around me
nature demands amends
spirit guides me
to take back the land
make amends
silence the cries of the lost
the lamentations
let them sleep forever sublime
knowing that we
have made a place
that can sustain us
a place of certainty
and sanctuary

58.

earth spirit
shout to raise
the living dead
each one
hear ancestors cry
mend the broken bones
wild damaged ones
earth spirit
know our wandering
our anguished offering
through time
earth spirit
reclaim soil soul seed
all the living green
help us surrender
that we may live again

59.

migrating birds
come rest here
teach us
all life follows
divine change
find pattern in structure
go true north
follow organic spirit
guided prophecy
hidden among growing things
that there may be hope
in these hills that there be renewal
that all living beings
may rise up
proclaiming pure delight
beauty that restores
beyond all manmade limitations
be welcomed

60.

wilderness within
wild woman
aging crone
wise hag
she who holds
mystery
stir the cauldron
tend the flames
bring life to fire
carry messages
from the future
a shroud of blackness
will cover the earth
sooted sorrow
so deep ash will fall like rain
heat rising
from unseen
burning

61.

lingering twilight
all-enveloping mist
that which is deep within us
rising
fugitive desire
in these lonesome hills
time loses meaning
fragments of past lives
hold hostage
the will to nurture growth
slaughter hope
against all sentient green
living beings
offering no escape
mountains dissolve
as earth slides into ruin

62.

harsh winter wind
again and again
soul deep snowfall
holding earth
shades of black and gray
among barren landscapes
the mind may know
a springtime of green coming
still in the present
the inescapable now
bitter cold buries secrets
put away
all promises of resurrection

63.

stark stolen sky
no birds in flight
in sight
no sign that lush
verdant life
lay abundant
here
war ravaged
our hills and mountains
burns flesh to ash
turns our water
against us
slaughters thirst
makes our
longings kill
all is black
coal black greed
no way to choose life
when greed
brings the constant
sound of death
calling away
deliverance

64.

daybreak
night falling
into blue shadow
gray streaks
as the trickster
chases memory
repeat
tell
the same stories
until the past
is left behind

65.

my world is green
wild green
green with no limits
big bold green
growing changing
celebrates the
green in things
all green goodness

66.

fire so hot
death so dry
just ready
to let loose
fierce heat
miles and miles
of flames
climbing hills and mountains
felling trees
calling all hearts
to burn and break
hold in memory
lifelines gone
a show of hands

Index of First Lines

again and again, 17
all fields, 29
all old souls, 60
autumn ending, 19

barren broken hill, 55
blackbirds, 63
bring Buddha, 33
burning body of love, 64
burning pain, 40

clouds dressed in gray, 34

daybreak, 74

earth spirit, 68
earth works, 14
equine whispering, 36

fierce grief shadows me, 67
fierce unyielding winds, 51
fierce winter cold, 44
fire so hot, 76
fly high, 54

go high up, 26

hard rain, 24
harsh winter wind, 72

hear them cry, 11
heavy heart, 52
here and there, 20

in the gray blue wash of dawn, 61

lingering twilight, 71
listen little sister, 16

mammoth caves, 46
migrating birds, 69
morning dawn, 38
mud sliding down, 22
my world is green, 75

night moves, 13
no crops grow, 21

on hallowed ground, 50
overlooking water, 56

pink and white oleander, 25

red beard, 57
renegades roam here, 62
returning to sacred places, 41
ritual places, 49

small horses ride me, 15
snow-covered earth, 18
softly treading black bear, 39
soil rich with lime, 35
sometimes falling rain, 32
stained black, 47
stark stolen sky, 73
star of david, 66
straight ahead, 27
sublime shadows of midnight, 37
such then is beauty, 12
sunken faces, 58

take the, 65
tap dancing, 43
the glory in old barns, 30
toward light, 48
turtle islands everywhere, 31

walking the long way home, 42
when the dawn, 53
when trees die, 28
wilderness within, 70
winds of fate, 45
wingspan wide, 23
with water, 59

Kentucky Voices

Miss America Kissed Caleb
Billy C. Clark

New Covenant Bound
T. Crunk

The Total Light Process: New and Selected Poems
James Baker Hall

Upheaval: Stories
Chris Holbrook

With a Hammer for My Heart: A Novel
George Ella Lyon

Famous People I Have Known
Ed McClanahan

Nothing Like an Ocean: Stories
Jim Tomlinson

Sue Mundy: A Novel of the Civil War
Richard Taylor

At The Breakers: A Novel
Mary Ann Taylor-Hall

Come and Go, Molly Snow: A Novel
Mary Ann Taylor-Hall

Buffalo Dance: The Journey of York
Frank X Walker

When Winter Come: The Ascension of York
Frank X Walker

The Cave
Robert Penn Warren